CONTENTS

BODY STRUCTURE

The Heart

page

6 Your heart - a special muscle
7 Inside your heart
8 Open and shut
9 Your hard working heart

BODY IN ACTION

How Does Your Heart Work?

10 A circular system
12 A one way journey
13 ...For special delivery
14 Dangerous ideas!
16 Your beating heart
18 Blood on the move
19 Your heart rate
20 What is your pulse?
21 The sound of your heart

HEALTH AND FITNESS

A Healthy Heart

22 Keeping in rhythm
23 Heart disease
24 Look after your heart - it's the only one you have
26 How to help

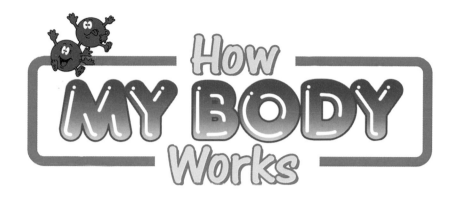

The
Heart

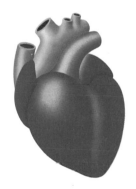

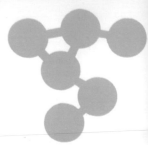

The Heart

Your heart - a special muscle

Your heart never rests. It started to beat before you were born and it will go on beating steadily throughout your life.

Your heart is made of a special type of muscle called cardiac muscle and it gets bigger as you grow. It's about the same size as your clenched fist, and weighs about 250 grams. If you place your fist against the centre of your chest with your knuckles pointing to your left side, you will feel your heart beating about once every second. Surrounded by your lungs and protected by your rib cage, your heart works like a powerful pump, sending blood to every part of your body.

Sometimes your heart changes its speed, by beating faster or slower, depending on how much oxygen your body needs.

Your heart is like a muscular bag, filled with blood. As the muscle contracts, it acts like a 'pump', pushing blood around your body.

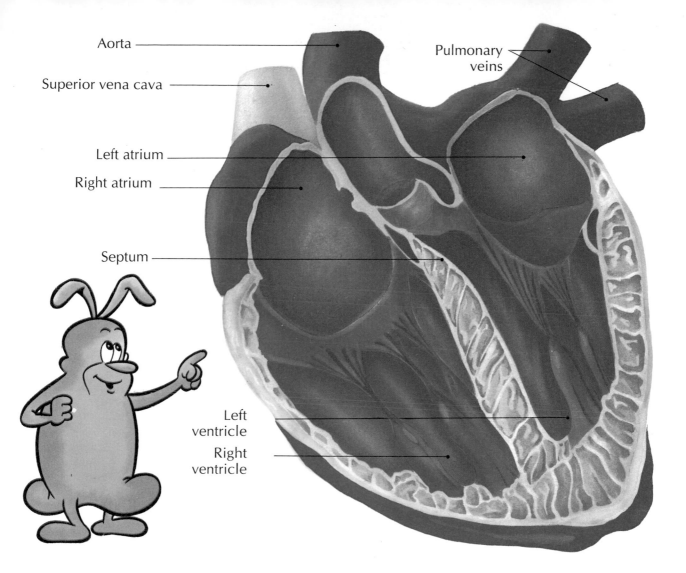

Aorta

Superior vena cava

Left atrium

Right atrium

Septum

Pulmonary veins

Left ventricle

Right ventricle

Inside your heart

Your heart is divided into two halves which lie to the right and left of each other, separated by a wall called the septum. Each half is made up of two parts: an upper chamber, the atruim, and a lower chamber, the ventricle.

The upper chambers fill with blood at the same time. Their thin muscular walls contract and squeeze blood into the lower chambers through valves which act like one way doors, closing firmly once the blood has passed through them.

When the ventricles are full of blood, they give a powerful squeeze and push blood into the arteries, the strong tubes that carry blood away from the heart.

The right side of your heart sends deoxygenated blood back to your lungs, for a fresh supply of oxygen. This 'fresh' blood then flows back to the left side of your heart to begin a new journey round your body.

The left ventricle has to pump blood all round your body. To give it extra strength, its muscular walls are thicker than those of the right ventricle.

Open and shut

Put your ear against a friend's chest and listen for a moment. You'll hear the 'lub-dup' sound of your friend's heart beating. But how does the heart actually make this sound?

Your heart has special valves which make sure that blood always flows in the same direction. The tricuspid valve separates the upper and lower chambers of the right side of your heart. The mitral valve does the same for the left. These valves open to allow blood to pass through, then close to stop it flowing backwards. As they close, they make the 'lub' sound.

Blood leaves the heart through a second set of valves. The 'dup' is the sound of these valves closing. After a brief silence, the 'lub-dup' starts again!

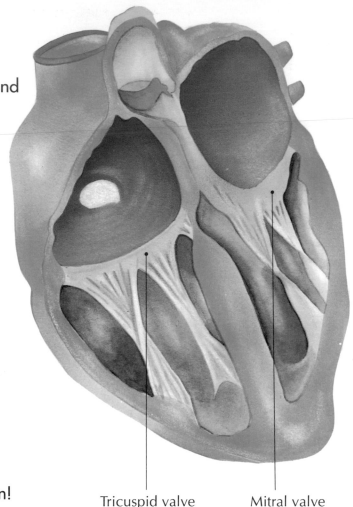

Tricuspid valve   Mitral valve

Plasmus is in love! He just has to look at his girlfriend to make his heart pound. Have you felt your heart beating faster? It often happens when you've been running. Your heart knows when your body needs more oxygen, so it works harder to pump blood faster to all your body organs.

YOUR HARD WORKING HEART

Your heart is a very powerful muscle. Just think of all the work it does. At rest, the average adult heart beats at a rate of 60-80 times a minute. A small child's heart beats faster, about 120 times a minute. As blood leaves the heart, it travels at a speed of about 30 centimetres per second. In one minute, five to seven litres of blood are pumped through your body. In one day your heart moves about 10,000 litres, pumping more than 200 million litres in a lifetime!

Heart rate: 60-80 per minute

Heart rate: 120 per minute

How Does Your Heart Work?

A circular system

Your heart is the centre of your body's transport system, pumping blood to every part of your body. This is called the circulation system. There are three main parts, or circuits, to your circulation system. One circuit connects your heart to your lungs. A second circuit

collects blood from the abdomen area and carries it to the liver, while the third circuit sends blood around the rest of your body and back again.

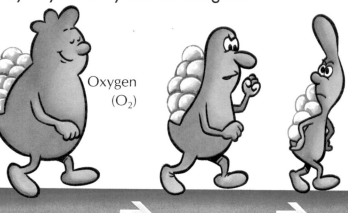

Oxygen (O$_2$)

Left atrium

Right atrium

BLOOD TRAVELS TO YOUR LUNGS AND BACK TO YOUR HEART

Carbon dioxide is exchanged for oxygen in the lungs

Carbon dioxide (CO$_2$)

Deoxygenated blood

The journey from the heart to the lungs and back again is called pulmonary circulation. First of all, blood carrying carbon dioxide collects in the right atrium (upper chamber), and is squeezed into the right ventricle (lower chamber). Then it is pumped to your lungs where, through thousands of tiny air sacs, carbon dioxide is exchanged for a fresh supply of oxygen. The oxygenated blood then flows back through the pulmonary veins to the left side of your heart.

Now your blood is pumped all over your body, delivering oxygen wherever it is needed. It picks up waste carbon dioxide and returns through your veins to the right side of your heart to begin its journey all over again.

Your heart is the centre of your circulation system. Start in the right atrium and trace the arrows with your fingers, to see the journey your blood makes as it is pumped to your lungs, back to your heart, then round your body and back again.

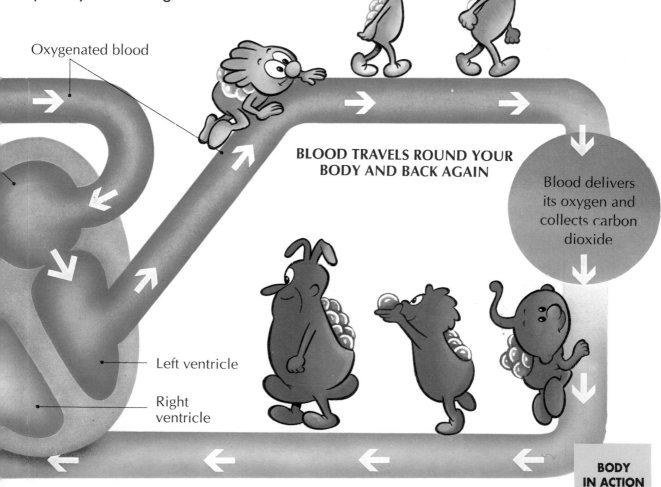

Oxygenated blood

BLOOD TRAVELS ROUND YOUR BODY AND BACK AGAIN

Blood delivers its oxygen and collects carbon dioxide

Left ventricle

Right ventricle

A one way journey

Blood carrying oxygen and carbon dioxide first enters your heart through the left and right upper chambers. These small cavities expand as blood fills them. When they contract, the blood pushes the flaps of the mitral and tricuspid valves open so that it can enter the lower chambers. Once the blood has passed through the valves, the flaps close so that blood cannot flow backwards. The two valves that control the blood leaving the lower chambers are called the semi-lunar valves. They act in a similar way, opening to allow blood to pass to the aorta on the left and the pulmonary artery on the right. Then they close to stop the blood from back-flowing.

CROSS SECTION OF A SEMI-LUNAR VALVE

Open

Closed

...For special delivery

The circulation system plays a vital role in the way your body works. Your blood acts like a delivery service, carrying oxygen, nutrients and antibodies to all parts of your body. Then it picks up waste products and carries them away to be filtered by organs such as the liver and kidneys. It's rather like your milkman who delivers milk to your door and collects your empty bottles so that they can be returned to the depot for cleaning and refilling!

Plasmus, Globus and Globina lead their friends, the red blood cells, on their journey through the heart. They have entered the right atrium and, as the tricuspid valve opens, they jump down into the right ventricle. Another squeeze and they will be pushed through a semi-lunar valve into the pulmonary artery on their way to the lungs to exchange carbon dioxide for oxygen. The valve shuts behind them so that they can only travel forwards. There's no going back in this one way system!

Dangerous ideas!

New ideas and discoveries about the way the body works have not always been welcomed. Over 400 years ago, a Flemish anatomist and doctor called Andreas Vesalius dissected dead bodies in order to study them. When he published his book in 1543, it contained the first accurate descriptions of human anatomy. The church did not accept his ideas and condemned him to death. It was the Holy Roman Emperor, Charles V, who saved him. Over 80 years later, in 1628, an English doctor, William Harvey, made an important discovery. He found that blood is pumped by the heart round the body in a circular movement. In 1660, an Italian doctor, Marcello Malpighi, used the new invention of the microscope to discover the fine capillaries which connect arteries to veins. This discovery confirmed Harvey's ideas about the circulation of the blood.

William Harvey

Andreas Vesalius

In 1531, the Spanish doctor, Michael Servetus discovered that blood circulates to the lungs from the right chamber of the heart. This discovery, together with his ideas about religion, led him to be condemned to death by the religious authorities in Geneva. He died at the stake in 1553, a victim of the unfairness of the times. Another Spaniard, Francesco Reina, completed Servetus' work on pulmonary circulation. This formed the foundation of William Harvey's discoveries about the role of the heart and blood circulation.

Your beating heart

Your heart does not always beat at the same rate; it adapts itself to your body's needs. When you are resting, your heart beats quite slowly, speeding up as you become more active. Your heart can double the number of beats per minute between resting and running.

Your heartbeat has two phases which affect the upper and lower chambers. The phase when your heart muscle has contracted fully and blood is squeezed out, is called systole. The second phase, when the heart relaxes and becomes full of blood once more is called diastole.

This is what happens during just one heartbeat:

1. The muscles of the heart's upper chambers contract and push the blood into the ventricles which are relaxed, (systole of the atriums; diastole of the ventricles).

2. The thick, muscular walls of the ventricles contract, the rising pressure snapping shut the valves which separate the upper and lower chambers. This makes the first sound you can hear in a heartbeat.

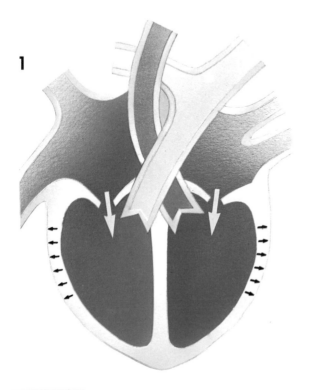

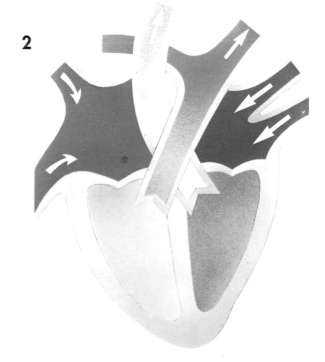

Globus can hardly believe that all this happens in less than a second - the time it takes for just one heartbeat.

3. The upper chambers are filling with blood coming from the body (right side, blue) and the lungs (left side, red). This is the diastole of the upper chambers. In the meantime, the lower chambers or ventricles are full of blood, ready to go to the lungs and main arteries. The semi-lunar valves are closed.

4. The ventricles contract and force the semi-lunar valves open. Blood leaves the ventricles and enters the main arteries. At the same time, blood flows into the relaxed upper chambers. As the ventricles relax, the pressure in the main arteries forces the semi-lunar valves shut, making the second sound of the heartbeat.

3

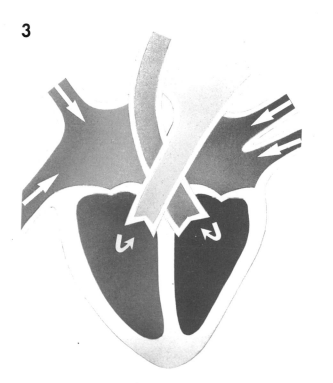

4

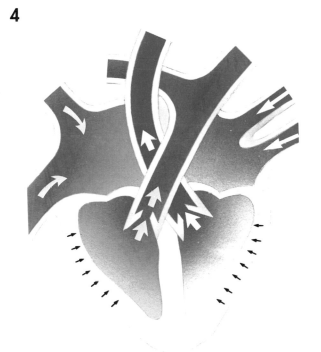

BLOOD ON THE MOVE

A human weighing 70 kilograms has about five litres of blood travelling at different rates inside the body. As blood leaves the heart, it's moving quite fast (30 centimetres per second). By the time it reaches the capillaries, it has slowed down to a gentle 0.3 centimetres per second. As blood is delivered back to the heart through the veins, it gradually speeds up again, moving at about 20 cm per second. The whole circuit takes less than a minute.

Red blood cells set off at great speed from the left side of the heart. Less than 60 seconds later, they've travelled right round the body.

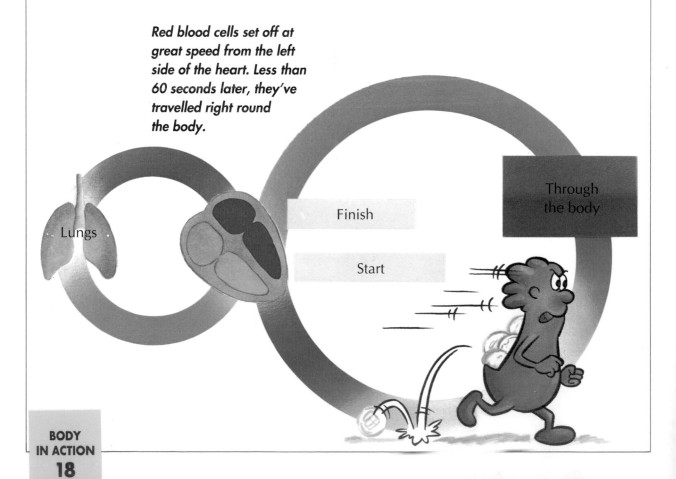

Lungs

Finish

Start

Through the body

Your heart rate

Your heart does not always beat at the same speed; lots of different things can affect it. Your heart rate will change when you're taking exercise. It will also change if you are excited or worried about something, or if you are ill with a high temperature. Your heart is very adaptable; it will always adjust its rate to new situations, beating faster or slower as necessary.

As you grow older, your heart rate slows down. A baby's heart beats at about 130 times per minute. Young children have a heart rate of between 100-120 beats a minute. An adult's average heart rate is almost half that speed, between 60-80 times per minute.

Heart rate:
25 per minute

Size can make quite a difference! The bigger the mammal, the slower the heart rate. The heart of a mouse beats at a rapid 600 times per minute, about 24 times faster than the heart of an elephant.

Heart rate:
70 per minute

Heart rate:
110 per minute

Heart rate:
600 per minute

What is your pulse?

Your pulse is the wave of blood that pushes through your arteries with each heartbeat. You can feel your pulse to discover how fast your heart is beating. Find the pulse on your wrist by using the tips of your middle three fingers. Gently press an artery against one of your wrist bones and count your pulse for 30 seconds. Double this figure and you will have the number of beats per minute.

Now jog on the spot for three minutes and take your pulse again. What has happened? Your heart rate will have increased because your heart beats faster when you are exercising. After a rest, you should find that it returns to normal. The fitter you are, the more quickly this happens.

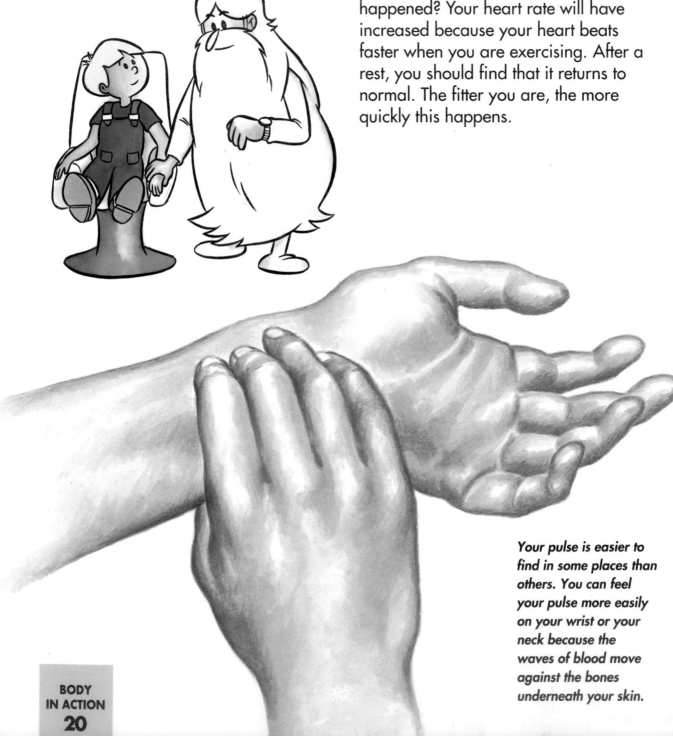

Your pulse is easier to find in some places than others. You can feel your pulse more easily on your wrist or your neck because the waves of blood move against the bones underneath your skin.

The sound of your heart

Doctors listen to your heart to make sure it's working normally. A special instrument called a stethoscope helps them to hear your heart more accurately. It's a Y-shaped tube. The arms of the Y fit inside the ears, while the base is connected to a thin, round piece which amplifies the sound that your heart makes. Doctors know exactly where to place the stethoscope on your body to hear your heart most clearly.

Although the valves in your heart open silently, they flap as they close. These flaps can be heard as sounds through your chest walls. A doctor can hear whether the valves are working properly through a stethoscope.

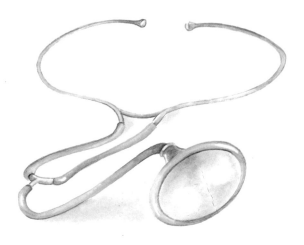

Stethoscope

The Professor wants to listen to his young patient's heart. He uses a stethoscope so that he can accurately hear the sound the heart makes and check that it's working normally.

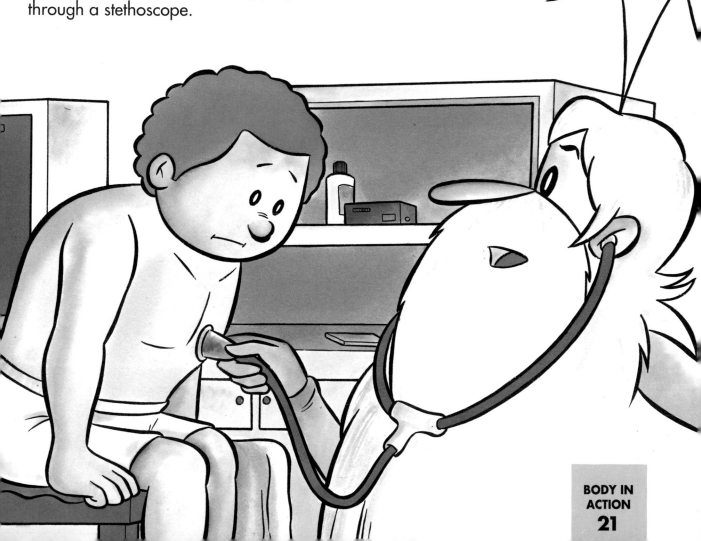

A Healthy Heart

Keeping in rhythm

A doctor can find out if something is wrong by listening to the way your heart 'ticks over'. It's rather like a car mechanic listening to an engine. If your heart is running too fast, it could be the result of an infection which raises your body temperature.

It's quite normal for your heart rate to increase as a result of exercise. If it varies when you are relaxed, a doctor will want to know what is wrong.

Changes in the heart rhythm have special names. An unusually rapid heartbeat is called tachycardia and an unusually slow heartbeat, bradycardia.

Doctors will always look for the reason why the heart is running too fast or too slowly. If the heart is not beating in a steady rhythm, it can mean that its pumping action is not working properly. Special drugs can help to put this right.

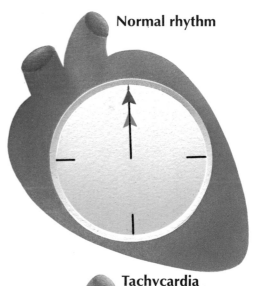

Normal rhythm

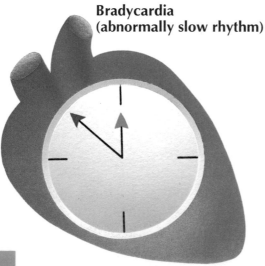

**Bradycardia
(abnormally slow rhythm)**

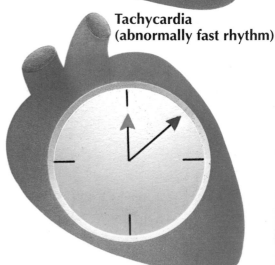

**Tachycardia
(abnormally fast rhythm)**

Heart disease

In the western world, heart disease kills more people than any other type of illness. It's worth looking for the reasons why because you can reduce the risk of heart disease.

As you grow older, the elastic fibres in your arteries begin to lose their ability to expand and contract. Sometimes they become 'furred up' so that blood cannot flow as easily as it should. This can lead to blockages, with serious results.

It's certainly worth doing something positive to make sure that you avoid having problems with your heart. Life can be very hectic. People rush about getting tired and angry as they cope with over-crowded trains or traffic jams. This leads to stress which, together with smoking and drinking, increase the risk of damage to your heart. If you begin a healthy lifestyle when you're young, you greatly improve your chances of having a fit and healthy heart.

Too little exercise and too much stress

Smoking tobacco and drinking alcohol

This man is creating problems for his heart. He's not looking after himself. He smokes and drinks too much, takes no exercise and doesn't take time off to relax. No wonder he's ended up in hospital!

Heart disease

Look after your heart - it's the only one you have

It's much better to prevent heart disease now than suffer from it later. If you start with good habits when you're young, it'll be easier to stick to them as you grow older. Just by keeping to a few simple rules, you'll give your heart the best possible chance of staying healthy.

1. Avoid too much fatty food and eat lots of fruit and vegetables.
2. Maintain your correct body weight by eating sensibly.
3. Say no to tobacco and alcohol.
4. Stop stress building up. Make sure there's time in your life for relaxation.
5. Take regular exercise. Remember that your heart is a muscle and needs exercise like any other part of your body.

Exercise is not only good for your body; it really helps you to relax. It also makes your heart stronger and improves your circulation.

There's no need to jog until you drop! Regular exercise for twenty minutes, three times a week, is a good basis for a healthy heart. You should take the sort of exercise that makes you breathe more deeply so that you can feel your heart beating faster. Do something that you really find enjoyable - it can be anything from a brisk walk to swimming, cycling, or even jogging!

There are worrying times in everyone's life. Have you ever left your homework until the last minute? Or stayed up late revising for an important exam? Try to build routines into your life so that you can organise your day for work and play, rest and relaxation.

How to help

It's important to act quickly when a person collapses. Find an adult to help you or call for an ambulance.

When guardsmen stand still for a long time, they sometimes faint. Standing still puts a strain on the valves in their veins. As they are not moving normally, the veins cannot send blood back to the heart at the usual rate. This means that the blood supply to the brain is reduced and it may cause them to faint.

If someone faints, find something to prop up their legs so that they are above the level of the head.

It's also important to loosen tight clothing such as collars and belts. Make sure the patient has plenty of fresh air and check to see if he's breathing properly.

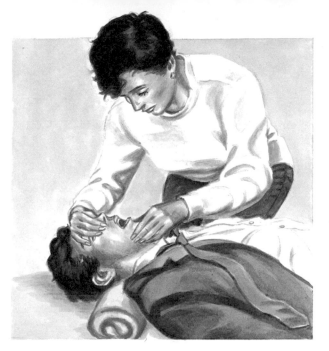

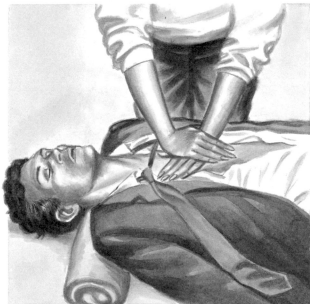

A heart attack is much more serious, as breathing stops if the heart stops beating. Help can be given, but never attempt it yourself. The best help you can give is to find an adult and call for an ambulance.

Mouth to mouth resuscitation can restore breathing. The patient's head is tilted backwards and the jaw pulled forward and upward to bring the tongue forward and ensure a clear airway. Check there is nothing in the mouth to cause an obstruction. The nostrils are pinched together and the mouth opened a little. Taking a deep breath, the helper puts his mouth over the patient's mouth and blows into the lungs, at a rate of one puff every five seconds. The patient's chest should rise as air enters the lungs. The helper must keep on blowing into the lungs until the patient starts breathing.

If there is no heartbeat or a pulse cannot be found, then heart massage could release blood into the circulation. It's done by pressing the heel of the hand onto the breast bone. The helper repeats this five times then pauses to give some more mouth to mouth resuscitation.

The Professor is always happy to be called out when he's needed because he knows the best way to help in an emergency. When you have done what you can, always get help as quickly as possible. Find an adult or call for help by making a free 999 emergency telephone call.

KEY WORDS

Anatomy – the study of the structure of the human body, including bones, joints, muscles, organs and other tissues. The study of how they work is called physiology.

Antibody – a substance that helps the body defend itself against infection.

Aorta – the main artery and largest blood vessel of the body.

Artery – a strong-walled vessel which carries blood away from the heart to different parts of the body.

Atriums – the upper chambers on each side of the heart.

Capillaries – tiny thin-walled vessels which carry oxygenated blood to every part of the body. They also collect carbon dioxide and other waste products for removal.

Carbon dioxide – a waste gas which is removed from body tissues in the blood and leaves the lungs as exhaled air.

Cardiac – describes things to do with the heart, for example cardiac muscle.

Circulation system – the way that blood moves around the body.

Diastole – when the chambers of the heart fill up with blood as part of the heart's momentary relaxation.

Pulmonary – to do with the lungs.

Stethoscope – an instrument for listening to noises inside the body, especially the heart and lungs. It was invented by Laennec, a French doctor, in 1816.

Systole – when the chambers contract as part of the heart's movement.

Vein – a blood vessel that carries blood back to the heart.

Ventricles – the two lower, pumping chambers of the heart.

HOW MY BODY WORKS

HOW MY BODY WORKS is an educational series that builds into a complete encyclopedia of the human body. Each volume introduces and explains one of its mysteries.

In Part 7 of How My Body Works, you've read all about your heart, the hardest working muscle in your body.

COMING IN PART 8 is the nerve control centre of your body, the brain.

READ ALL ABOUT:
● **How your brain receives** messages, processes information and controls your body's responses in only one thousandth of a second.
● **How your nerves transmit** messages as electric impulses to and from the brain.

Albert Barillé, (pictured left) is the author of this fascinating series of books. The human body is a series of complex systems and mechanisms, so to make it easier for you to understand how the body works, Barillé created The Professor, Captain Courageous, Globus, Toxicus and Virulus, plus many other colourful cartoon characters, to show you around. The Professor and his friends guide you through the body, explaining how it works in a clear and simple way that makes it fun.

PARTS OF YOUR MODEL
This will help you to identify all the pieces that go together to make your model.

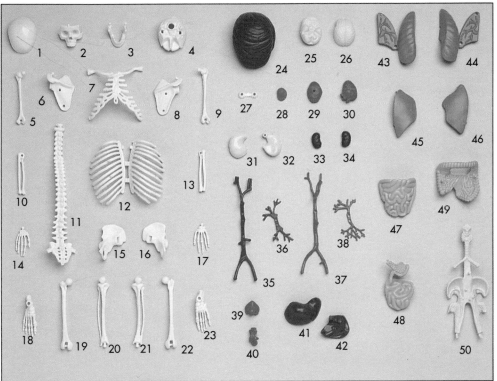

Published by
ORBIS PUBLISHING,
Griffin House,
161 Hammersmith Road,
London W6 8SD

BACK ISSUES
Back issues can be obtained by placing an order with your newsagent or, in case of difficulty, from our back numbers department. All cheques/postal orders should be made payable to Orbis Publishing Ltd.

BACK ISSUE CHARGES
Volume 1:
UK: 99p plus £1.00 p&p;
Eire: IR£0.99 plus £1.00 p&p
Thereafter:
UK: £2.99 plus 50p p&p;
Eire: IR£3.50 plus 50p p&p

**ADDRESS FOR
BACK ISSUES:**
Orbis Publishing Ltd, Unit 10, Wheel Lane Business Park, Wheel Lane, Westfield, Hastings, East Sussex, TN35 4SG. Tel: 0424 755755

BACK ISSUES OVERSEAS
Please place requests for copies of back issues with your newsagent or, in case of difficulty, please write to the relevant address given:

Australia
Gordon and Gotch Ltd, PO Box 290, Burwood VIC 3125 (Enclose cover price plus $1 p&h per issue)

New Zealand
Gordon and Gotch (NZ) Ltd, PO Box 584, Auckland.
Malta, Singapore & South Africa Back numbers are available at cover price from your newsagent.

© Procidis Albert Barillé
© 1992 Orbis Publishing Ltd, London
N7 92 12 17
Printed in Italy
by Officine Grafiche
De Agostini, Novara

1 Cranium
2 Front of skull
3 Jawbone
4 Back of skull

5 Left humerus
6 Left shoulder blade
7 Sternum
8 Right shoulder blade
9 Right humerus

10 Left radius and ulna
11 Spinal column
12 Rib-cage
13 Right radius and ulna

14 Bones of right hand
15 Right pelvis
16 Left pelvis
17 Bones of left hand

18 Bones of right foot
19 Femur
20 Right tibia and fibula
21 Left tibia and fibula
22 Femur
23 Bones of left foot

24 Scalp
25 Top part of brain
26 Bottom part of brain

27 Eyes

28 Pancreas
29 Front of heart
30 Back of heart

31 Front of stomach
32 Back of stomach
33 Right kidney
34 Left kidney

35 Principal veins
36 Pulmonary arteries
37 Principal arteries
38 Pulmonary veins

39 Bladder

40 Anal passage
41 Front of liver
42 Back of liver

43 Right lung
44 Left lung
45 Right pleura
46 Left pleura

47 Front of small intestine
48 Back of small intestine
49 Large intestine

50 Windpipe, gullet and cavities for the kidneys